Learning Tree
1 2 3

Paper

By Peter Stroud
Illustrated by Mike Lacey

Geddes+
Grosset

Read this book and see if you can answer the questions
and do the experiments. Ask an adult or an older friend to
help you and to tell you if your answers are right. Often
there is more than one answer to a question.

First published in hardback 1991
Copyright © Cherrytree Press Ltd 1991

This paperback edition first published 1991 by
Geddes & Grosset Ltd
David Dale House
New Lanark ML11 9DJ

ISBN 1 85534 456 4

Printed and bound in Italy by L.E.G.O. s.p.a., Vicenza

Lots of different things are made of paper.
How many can you think of?
Are they made of the same sort of paper?

Some paper is soft.
We wrap delicate things in soft paper.
We mop up water with soft paper.
Tissues and nappies are made of soft paper.

Some paper is thick and strong.
Look at paper bags and sacks.
Look at boxes and cartons made of cardboard.
Cardboard is very strong paper.
Paper money is strong too.

The most important use of paper is for writing
and reading.
We can write or print on paper.
Books and newspapers are printed by machines.

Look at different kinds of paper.
Lined paper is for writing on.
What kind of paper has holes down the sides?
What kind of paper can you see through?

Paper is made from trees.
The wood is sawn and chopped into tiny chips.

The chips are mixed with water and chemicals.
This mixture is called wood pulp.

The wood pulp is poured out in a thin layer.
When it is dry, it goes through a big roller.

It goes through more and more rollers.
They make it thin and smooth.

Trees take a long time to grow.
Millions of them are cut down every day.
It takes a lot of trees to make the paper for one
day's newspapers.

People who waste paper are wasting trees.
New paper can be made from old paper.
Collect your waste paper.
Find out if it can be recycled.

Paper soaks up water.
It goes soggy and loses its strength.
Test different kinds of paper.
See which ones go soggy first.
Milk cartons are made of paper.
Can you see why they do not go soggy?

Tear some old paper into pieces.
Soak them in water overnight.
Strain the soggy mush in the morning.
Mix it with glue or flour-and-water paste.

This mixture is called papier mâché.
You can use it to make models.

Shape your papier mâché while it is soft.
Try making a bowl or a pot or a statue.
Leave your models to dry and harden.
Then paint them.

You can make a mask with strips of paper.
Find a dish the size of your face.
Turn it over and cover it with vaseline.

Soak strips of paper until they are soft.
Cover the dish with one layer of strips.
Leave holes for your eyes.

Build up layers of strips and paste.
Shape a nose or horns as you build.
Then leave your mask to dry and paint it.

Paper is easy to cut.
Cut out shapes to make a picture.
A picture made from cut-out shapes is called a collage.

Draw a spiral and colour it like a snake.
Cut it out and hang it up.

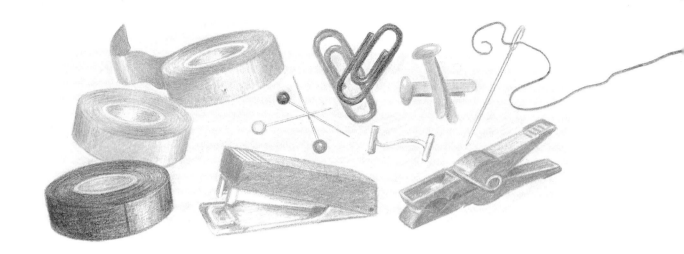

You can stick paper with glue.
How many other ways can you fasten it?

Make some paper chains.
How will you fasten your paper strips?

A flat sheet of paper is flimsy.
You can make it strong by rolling it up.
You can make a skeleton for your models.
Cover your skeleton with papier mâché.

You can make shapes by folding paper.
Fold a sheet of newspaper into a hat.
Make a snake from two strips of paper.
Glue on a head and tail.

Make your own book.
Fold the sheets of paper.
Staple or sew the pages together.
Write your book and draw the pictures.

More about paper

The first paper
Paper was invented in China about 2000 years ago. The Chinese used paper for writing letters, and for making lists of farm animals and crops. The Chinese also invented paper money. They made the first banknotes about 1000 years ago.

Making paper
Paper can be made from all sorts of plants. In the past, paper was made from bamboo, straw, rice, grass, flax and sugar cane. It was even made from old rags.

Today, paper is mostly made from trees. The pulp is treated with bleach to make it white. Then, some of the paper is coloured with dye.

Look at paper
Collect paper of different kinds and colours. What can you tell by looking at the different sorts? Rub them with your finger. Can you feel differences? Look at the surface of the paper through a magnifying glass? Can you see the fibres the paper is made from?

Look at a newspaper and a colour magazine? The magazine paper is smoother. Photographs look glossier when they are printed on shiny paper.

Paper plus
You can stop paper soaking up water by coating it. Milk and juice cartons do not go soggy because they are made from paper that has been waterproofed. Waterproof cartons have a coating of wax or a lining of plastic or metal foil.

You can make paper stronger by adding more layers to it. Cardboard often has three layers. A layer of corrugated paper (folded into a zigzag) is sandwiched between two boards.

You can make paper more useful by adding other things to it. You can smooth wood with sandpaper. The paper has a layer of sand stuck to it. What other things are stuck to paper?

1

1 Can you find three different kinds of paper?

2 What kind of paper do you blow your nose on?

3 Name two things made from strong paper.

4 Which of these is paper made from: stones, scrap metal or trees?

5 What kinds of paper are these?

2

6 Why does writing paper have lines ruled on it?

7 Which one of these is the odd one out: book, newspaper, ruler, photograph, magazine? Why?

8 Is wet paper heavier or lighter than dry paper?

9 Is wet paper stronger than dry?

10 What is brown paper used for?

11 What sort of paper can you eat?

12 What is silver paper? Is it made from paper?

13 Where was paper invented?

14 Why do banknotes need to be so strong?

15 Name five ways of fastening two pieces of paper together.

3

16 Make a book from paper. Sew the pages together or use a long stapler.

17 Use your book as a notebook. Write the answers to these questions in it. Think of questions you would like to ask about paper. Write those in the book too.

18 What is the best thing to do with waste paper? Should you throw it away, burn it or recycle it?

19 Why is sticky paper sticky?

20 What kind of paper would you use to wrap a parcel, a sandwich, a glass vase?

21 Would it be sensible to make a vase out of papier mâché? What would happen when you filled it with water? Use papier mâché to make something useful.

22 Why does the milk not make the milk carton soggy?

23 What did people write on before paper was invented?

24 Find out what *papyrus* is.

25 Find out what *origami* is.

26 Why is more paper made in Canada than in Africa?

27 Do you think you could make a whole house of paper?

28 Find out which countries produce most paper. Do those countries have big forests?

29 Patterned paper is used for wrapping paper and for wallpaper. Make a design for a sheet of wrapping paper. Will the same design make a good wallpaper?

Index